Rock 'n Roll Review

150 trivia Questions and Answers

3R Series – Review, Recognize and Remember

James Magee

Published by Novel Characters, 444 North Paula Drive, Suite 334, Dunedin, FL 34698

First paperback printing was in 2011.

The aim of this book . . .

Rock 'n Roll Review will be the nineth book in a series of books subtitled Review-Remember-Recognize. The first book is titled American History. The second book was titled World History. The third and fourth books were respectively titled The Constitution of the United State and Classic Novels (Authors and their Titles) . The sixth and seventh books were respectively titled Who Wrote this Book? and Art History Review. The eighth book was Music History Review. The 150 questions and answers in this book discuss the major singers along with the personalities that surrounded this unique art form.

This work examines a sample of the most well-known and respected rock 'n roll songs from the start of the modern phenomena known as Rock 'n Roll.. Since each question is randomly chosen, the book can be opened to any page at any time.

Most of the research in this book is from Wikipedia.

"I don't think rock & roll should be analyzed or even thought about deeply."

Keith Richards

QUESTION # 1

Which group (singer) sang **"Little Girl of Mine"**? Was it The Dell Vikings, The Cleftones or The Diamonds?

QUESTION # 2

Which group (singer) sang **"Little Darlin'"**? Was it The Cleftones, The Diamonds or The Dell-Vikings?

ANSWER # 1

"Little Girl of Mine" was sung by The Cleftones. This doo-wop group was formed in 1955 at Jamaica High School in Queens, New York. This quintet was originally called The Silvertones. Beside this song, the group initially charted "You, Baby, You," "Can't We Be Sweethearts," and "Heart and Soul."

ANSWER # 2

"Little Darlin'" was sung by The Diamonds. When this Canadian group's lead singer, Stan Fisher, was unable to perform one night because of a law exam, their manager, Dave Somerville, replaced him to rave reviews that permanently established the future of the group.

QUESTION # 3

Which group (singer) sang **"Come Go With Me"**?   Was it The Dell Vikings, The Cleftones or The Diamonds?

QUESTION # 4

Which group (singer) sang **"Tonight (Could Be The Night)"**?   Was it The Eternals, The Velvets or The Jive Five?

ANSWER # 3

"**Come Go With Me**" was sung by The Dell Vikings. Also known as the Del-Vikings, this racially integrated group's name came from the Norse Vikings, the Vikings baseball club from Brooklyn sponsored by Nathans, or the Viking Press. The Del or Dell is a tribute to the rock and roll group by that name.

ANSWER # 4

"**Tonight (Could Be The Night)**" was sung by The Velvets. This African-American quintet from Odessa, West Texas was formed by Virgil Johnson – a high school teacher – with four of his students. Roy Orbinson heard them and signed them to a record label in 1960.

QUESTION # 5

Which group (singer) sang **"Angel Baby"**?
Was it Rosie & The Originals, Kathy Young
& The Innocents or Leslie Gore?

QUESTION # 6

Which group (singer) sang **"Silhouettes"**?
Was it The Penguins, The Flamingos or The
Rays?

ANSWER # 5

"**Angel Baby**" was sung by Rosie and The Originals. While attending Mission Bay High School in San Diego, 14 year old Rosie Hamlin wrote the lyrics for this song as a poem. Eventually, she became entangled in a legal battle involving royalties over copyright infringement that lasted for years.

ANSWER # 6

"**Silhouettes**" was sung by The Rays. This single by a Philadelphia vocal group eventually soared to #3 on the Billboard Top 100. In time, the Canadian pop group, The Diamonds, also had a successful version along with a version by the British Invasion group, Herman's Hermits.

QUESTION # 7

Which group (singer) sang **"Oh What A Night"**?   Was it The Dells, The Flamingoes or The Penguins?

QUESTION # 8

Which group (singer) sang **"The Closer You Are"**?   Was it The Passions, Earl Wilson & The Channels or The Impalas?

ANSWER # 7

"**Oh What A Night**" was sung by The Dells. This Chicago suburb vocal group was formed in 1952 by a group of teenagers. Their other great hit was "Stay In My Corner." One of the longest running vocal groups, The Dells were backup for Della Washington from 1961 to 1962.

ANSWER # 8

"**The Closer You Are**" was sung by Earl Lewis & The Channels. The original Channels had two members from The Lotharios as replacements. While three members sang three-part harmony, another rounded out the bottom and Earl Wilson led and added his falsetto voice.

QUESTION # 9

Which group (singer) sang **"There's A Moon Out Tonight"**?   Was it Tommy Edwards, The Five Satins or The Capris?

QUESTION # 10

Which group (singer) sang **"That's My Desire"**?   Was it Dion & The Belmonts, The Shirelles or Marta and the Vandellas?

ANSWER # 9

"**There's A Moon Out Tonight**" was sung by The Capris. High school teenagers from Franklin K. Laine, Woodrow Wilson and John Adams joined together in Ozone Park, Queens in 1957 to form this group. They adopted their name from the 1957 Lincoln Capri car by that name – not the island.

ANSWER # 10

"**That's My Desire**" was sung by Dion & The Belmonts. Dion DiMucci was the lead singer of this Bronx vocal group named after Belmont Avenue in the Bronx. Dion escaped death with Buddy Holly, Richie Valens and J. P. "The Big Bopper" Richardson on Feb. 3rd, 1959 because he could not afford the $36.

QUESTION # 11

Which group (singer) sang **"That'l Be The Day"**? Was it Buddy Holly, Roy Orbinson or Conway Twitty?

QUESTION # 12

Which group (singer) sang **"Everyday Of The Week"**? Was it The Coasters, The Students or Frankie Lymon & The Teenagers? ?

ANSWER # 11

"That'l Be The Day" was sung by Buddy Holly. Born Charles Hardin Holley, this singer/songwriter from Lubbock, Texas married a secretary, Maria Elena Santiago, from Puerto Rico shortly after their first date. Now, she is a divorcee (her second husband) and grandmother living in Dallas, Texas.

ANSWER # 12

"Everyday Of The Week" was sung by The Students. This B-side of the original 1958 record eventually became the same music for the Dovel's hit "The Bristol Stomp." Stealing was not uncommon then. The raw and powerful voice of the lead singer fooled some listeners that it was Frankie Lymon singing.

QUESTION # 13

Which group (singer) sang **"Remember When"**?   Was it Earl Lewis & The Channels, The Diamonds or Larry Chance & The Earls?

QUESTION # 14

Which group (singer) sang **"My Girl"**?   Was it The Temptations, The Cleftones or Smoky Robinson & The Miracles?

ANSWER # 13

"**Remember When**" was sung by Larry Chance & The Earls. Before moving to the Bronx and being discovered with The Earls on a corner in front of a subway station, Larry Chance attended a Philadelphia high school with Chubby Checker and Frankie Avalon.

ANSWER # 14

"**My Girl**" was sung by The Temptations. This Motown group out of Detroit, Michigan that was formed in 1960 as The Elgins always consisted of at least five male vocalists. Besides original member, Otis Williams, Eddie Kendricks, David Ruffin and three others were inducted into the Hall of Fame.

QUESTION # 15

Which group (singer) sang **"Earth Angel"**?
Was it The Rays, The Penguins or The
Jesters?

QUESTION # 16

Which group (singer) sang **"Just To Be With
You"**?   Was it The Passions, The Cleftones
or Little Anthony & The Imperials?

ANSWER # 15

"**Earth Angel**" was sung by The Penguins. This Los Angeles based group formed in 1953, who thought they were "cool" named themselves after the cartoon advertizing figure for Kool cigarettes – Willie the Penguin. Like The Orioles, The Flamingoes, and The Crows, they had a "bird" name.

ANSWER # 16

"**Just To Be With You**" was sung by The Passions. This Bensonhurst Brooklyn group, who were neighborhood friends of the The Mystics, also recorded the faster paced "I Only Want You," and "This Is My Love." "This Is My Love" is often referred to as Sweeter than – which is its opening lines.

QUESTION # 17

Which group (singer) sang **"Sorry (I Ran All The Way Home)"**? Was it The Students, The Impalas or The Coasters?

QUESTION # 18

Which group (singer) sang **"The Lion Sleeps Tonight"**? Was it The Penguins, The Monotones or The Tokens?

ANSWER # 17

"**Sorry (I Ran All The Way Home)**" was sung by The Impalas. The Impalas were an integrated group formed in 1958 with lead singer Joe "Speedo" Frazier as the only African American member. They recorded follow-ups like "Oh What A Fool" and an album before disbanding in 1961.

ANSWER # 18

"**The Lion Sleeps Tonight**" was sung by The Tokens. When this group formed in 1955 at Brooklyn's Abraham Lincoln High School, Neil Sedaka was an original member. When Jay Siegel became lead singer in 1956, the group had its first single, "While I Dream."

QUESTION # 19

Which group (singer) sang **"Little Star"**?
Was it Vito Picone & The Elegants, The
Penguins or The Capris?

QUESTION # 20

Which group (singer) sang **"Once In
Awhile"**? Was it Earl Lewis & The
Channels, Lenny & The Chimes or Lenny
Chance & Earls?

ANSWER # 19

"Little Star" was sung by Vito Picone & The Elegants. This South Beach, Staten Island group formed in 1956 usually performed informally under the Boardwalk beside their homes. Their nursery rhyme inspired song based on "Twinkle Twinkle Little Star" was co-wrote by Vito Picone and Arthur Venosa.

ANSWER # 20

"Once In A While" was sung by Lenny &The Chimes. This a'cappella Brooklyn street corner group which formed in 1959 was originally known as the Capris until they learned that friends of theirs from Ozone Park, Queens had already chosen that name. This song was a 1937 Tommy Dorsey hit.

QUESTION # 21

Which group (singer) sang **"You Were Mine"**?   Was it The Moonglows, The Coasters or The Fireflies?

QUESTION # 22

Which group (singer) sang **"Tonight, Tonight"**?   Was it The Mellow-Kings, Larry Chance & Earls or Earl Wilson & The Channels?

ANSWER # 21

"You Were Mine" was sung by The
Fireflies. This Philadelphia doo-wop group
debuted with "The Crawl" which was
followed by their hit "You Were Mine."
After "I Can't Say Goodbye," they disbanded
only to reunite+ in 1962 with the single "You
Were Mine for Awhile."

ANSWER # 22

"Tonight, Tonight" was sung by The
Mellow Kings. This quintet from Mount
Vernon, NY was originally known as the
Mellotones until they realized the name had
already been taken. When the lead singer,
Bob Scholl, died in a boat accident, his
brother, Jerry, started it back up again.

QUESTION # 23

Which group (singer) sang **"Bobalu's Wedding Day"**?   Was it Smoky Robinson & The Miracles, The Eternals or Little Anthony & The Imperials?

QUESTION # 24

Which group (singer) sang **"Wild One"**? Was it Freddie Cannon, Chubby Checker or Bobby Rydell?

ANSWER # 23

"**Bobalu's Wedding Day**" was sung by The Eternals. The Eternals were a Bronx group who formed in Junior High School who were known first as The Gleamers and then as The Orbits. Their first novelty hit "Rockin In The Jungle" was followed by another novelty hit, "Bobalu's Wedding Day."

ANSWER # 24

"**Wild One**" was sung by Bobby Rydell. He was born Robert Louis Ridarelli in Philadelphia, PA. when he was a drummer in the band, Rocco & The Saints, alongside Frankie Avalon. "Wild One" followed his first two hits: "Kissin' Time" and "We Got Love."

QUESTION # 25

Which group (singer) sang **"Party Doll"**?
Was it Buddy Knox, Buddy Holly or Bobby
Freeman?

QUESTION # 26

Which group (singer) sang **"I've Had It"**?
Was it The Ventures, The Bell Notes or
Duane Eddy?

ANSWER # 25

"**Party Doll**" was sung by Buddy Knox. Born in Happy, Texas, Buddy was recorded because of a fellow Texan, Roy Orbinson – whose band was known as "The Teen Kings" After this hit charted at #1, he followed it with a #17 hit called "Rock Your Baby To Sleep," and a #9 hit called "Hula Love."

ANSWER # 26

"**I've Had I**" was sung by The Bell Notes. This group from Long Island, New York regularly performed in a Bronx bar where the owner's son and Steven Tyler would entertain between The Bell Notes' sets. Steven Tyler would later become famous as the lead for the band Aerosmith.

QUESTION # 27

Which group (singer) sang **"Sh-Boom"**?
Was it The Silhouettes, The Five Satins or
The Chords?

QUESTION # 28

Which group (singer) sang **"Donna"**? Was it
Richie Valens, Frankie Avalon or Ricky
Nelson?

ANSWER # 27

"**Sh-Boom**" was sung by The Chords. While this group formed in the Bronx, it was not discovered until 3 years later in a subway station. The words "Yadda da da yadda da da da da da" were never sung in the original even though "The Crew-Cuts" added them in their version.

ANSWER # 28

"**Donna**" was sung by Richie Valens (born Ricardo Esteban Valenzuela Reyes). Leading the Chicano rock movement, his hit song "La Bamba" is a Mexican folk song with a rock rhythm. His career ended on Feb. 3rd, 1959 along with Buddy Holly and J. P. "The Big Bopper" Richardson in a plane crash.

QUESTION # 29

Which group (singer) sang **"Honeycomb"**? Was it Paul Anka, Jimmie Rogers or Pat Boone?

QUESTION # 30

Which group (singer) sang **"Tallahassee Lassie"**? Was it Jerry Lee Lewis, Johnny Horton or Freddie Cannon?

ANSWER # 29

"**Honeycomb**" was sung by James Frederick "Jimmie" Rodgers. Recorded in 1957, his greatest hit, which stayed on the top of the charts for four weeks, was followed by such hits as: "Kisses Sweeter Than Wine," "Oh-Oh, I'm Falling In Love Again," "Secretly," and "Sloop John B."

ANSWER # 30

"**Tallahassee Lassie**" was sung by Freddie Cannon. Born Frederick Picariello, he grew up in the North Boston suburb of Lynn, MA. Of his 22 charted songs over 4 decades, the most notable were "Way Down Yonder in New Orleans," "Chattanooga Shoe Shine Boy," and "Muskrat Scramble."

QUESTION # 31

Which group (singer) sang **"Since I Fell For You"**?   Was it Jan & Dean, Lenny Welsh or The Beach Boys?

QUESTION # 32

Which group (singer) sang **"There Goes My Baby"**?   Was it The Temptations, Smoky Robinson & The Miracles or The Drifters?

ANSWER # 31

"**Since I Fell For You**" was sung by Lenny Welch. Lenny Welch was born Leon Welch in New York City and raised in Asbury Park, New Jersey. This big band standard reached #4 on the U. S. Hot Billboard 100. Besudes recording the first vocal version of "A Taste of Honey," his other hit was "Ebb Tide."

ANSWER # 32

"**There Goes My Baby**" was sung by The Drifters. Besides splinter groups, there have been 60 vocalists in the Treadwell Drifter group between 1953 and 1963. The two most notable lead singers for the Drifters have been Clyde McPhatter (from Bill Ward & The Dominoes) and Ben E. King.

QUESTION # 33

Which group (singer) sang "**Rock Around the Clock**"? Was it Bill Haley & The Comets, Little Richard or Jerry Lee Lewis?

QUESTION # 34

Which group (singer) sang "**You Send Me**"? Was it Jackie Wilson, Sam Cooke or Tommy Edwards?

ANSWER # 33

"**Rock Around the Clock**" was sung by Bill Haley & the Comets. From 1954 to 1956, this group would have 9 hit singles in the Top 20. One would be #1 while 3 others would be in the Top 10. A movie names after this song would feature The Platters and the famous radio disc-jockey, Alan Freed.

ANSWER # 34

"**You Send Me**" was sung by Sam Cooke. The King of Soul had 29 Top 40 hits between 1957 and 1964 and was second to Elvis in record sales. Some of his hits were: "Bring It On Home To Me," "Chain Gang," "Wonderful World," "A Change Is Coming," and "Twistin The Night Away."

QUESTION # 35

Which group (singer) sang **"Tears On My Pillow"**? Was it Frankie Lymon & The Teenagers, Little Anthony & The Imperials or The Cleftones?

QUESTION # 36

Which group (singer) sang **"Maybe Baby"**? Was it The Capris, The Paragons or Buddy Holly & The Crickets?

ANSWER # 35

"**Tears On My Pillow**" was sung by Little Anthony & The Imperials. When members of the Chesters joined Anthony Gourdine from the Duponts in 1958, they formed a New York group called the Imperials. In time, DJ Alan Freed gave Gourdine the name "Little Anthony."

ANSWER # 36

"**Maybe Baby**" was sung by Buddy Holly & The Crickets. Buddy Holly's ambitions led to the split with the Crickets who wanted to leave NY and go back to Lubbock, TX. Because his manager, Norman Petty, withheld his royalties, he was forced to go on the road to pay his bills. Thus, the tragic end.

QUESTION # 37

Which group (singer) sang **"It's Only Make Believe"**?   Was it Conway Twitty, Jimmy Clanton or Bobby Helms?

QUESTION # 38

Which group (singer) sang **"Personality"**? Was it Freddie Cannon, Lloyd Price or Jackie Wilson?

ANSWER # 37

"It's Only Make Believe" was sung by Conway Twitty. Named Harold Lloyd Jenkins after the silent screen actor by his great uncle, this Mississippian baseball player missed the Philadelphia Phillies draft because of Uncle Sam's draft. Sam Phillips of Sun Records helped with the "right" sound.

ANSWER # 38

"Personality" was sung by Lloyd Price. Known as "Mr. Personality," he was born in a suburb of New Orleans. Fats Domino played piano in his backup band when he recorded the massive hit "Lawdy Miss Clawdy." They also recorded a smaller hit titled "Oooh, oooh, oooh."

QUESTION # 39

Which group (singer) sang "**Handy Man**"?
Was it Sam Cooke, Clyde McPhatter or
Jimmy Jones?

QUESTION # 40

Which group (singer) sang "**Over The
Rainbow**"?   Was it The Dimensions, The
Mellow Kings or The Fireflies?

ANSWER # 39

"**Handy Man**" was sung by Jimmy Jones. This singer/songwriter African American Alabaman sang in a smooth, yet soulful falsetto. When the flutist failed to show up for the recording of this 1960 hit, his partner whistled the part. Another of his hits was "Good Timin'."

ANSWER # 40

"**Over The Rainbow**" was sung by The Dimensions. It was the #1 song on the charts in 1961. The lead singer and arranger was Lenny Dell who continues to entertain the public on his own with his exceptionally gifted voice in nightclubs and other venues.

QUESTION # 41

Which group (singer) sang **"My Special Angel"**?   Was it Bobby Freeman, Bobby Helms or Bobby Knox?

QUESTION # 42

Which group (singer) sang **"Twilight Time"**?   Was it The Duprees, The Skyliners or The Platters?

ANSWER # 41

"**My Special Angel**" was sung by Bobby
Helms. This crossover hit in 1957 rose to #7
on the Billboard Hot 100. It was recorded by
Bobby Vinton and Frankie Avalon in 1963.
It was revived in1968 by the Pennsylvania
vocal group, The Vogues, who had soared to
the Top Ten with "Five O'Clock World."

ANSWER # 42

"**Twilight Time**" was sung by The Platters.
Tony Williams and Sonny Turner were the
lead singers for this group. Zola Taylor –
who was the second of three wives of Frankie
Lymon – sang with The Platters from 1954 to
1962 when they had most of their hit singles.

QUESTION # 43

Which group (singer) sang **"It's All In The Game"**?   Was it Jerry Butler, Tommy Edwards or Brook Benton?

QUESTION # 44

Which group (singer) sang **"Who's Sorry Now"**?   Was it Connie Francis, Brenda Lee or Leslie Gore?

ANSWER # 43

"**It's All In The Game**" was sung by
Tommy Edwards. Singer/songwriter
Virginian died at age 47 from a brain
aneurysm. This song was written in 1912 by
then future Vice-President Charles G. Dawes
under the title "A Melody in A Major" with
lyrics added in 1951.

ANSWER # 44

"**Who's Sorry Now**" was sung by Connie
Francis (Concetta Rose Maria Franconero).
Her other hits were: "Where The Boys Are,"
"Lipstick On Your Collar," "Stupid Cupid,"
"Everybody's Somebody's Fool," etc. Later,
in life she admitted her love for Bobby Darin
who had married Sandra Dee.

QUESTION # 45

Which group (singer) sang **"When"**?   Was it The Everly Brothers, The Kalin Twins or Simon & Garfunkel?

QUESTION # 46

Which group (singer) sang **"Teen Angel"**? Was it Frankie Avalon, Ricky Nelson or Mark Dinning?

ANSWER # 45

"When" was sung by The Kalin Twins. This duo who hailed from Port Jervis, New York had a couple of recording flops before recording this one-hit wonder that climbed the charts to the #5 slot in 1958. The twins, Harold (Hal) and Herbert (Herb) then recorded "Forget Me Not."

ANSWER # 46

"Teen Angel" was sung by Mark Dinning. Teen idol Oklahoman Max E. Dinning recorded this hit in 1960. The lyrics were written by his sister, Jean, and her husband, Red Surrey. Speaking of the death of a teenage love, they proved to be too morbid for many UK radio stations. He died of a heart attack at age 52.

QUESTION # 47

Which group (singer) sang **"Sincerely"**?
Was it The Moonglows, The Five Satins or
The Capris?

QUESTION # 48

Which group (singer) sang **"Chantilly
Lace"**? Was it The Fleetwoods, J. P. "The
Big Bopper" Richardson or Freddie Cannon?

ANSWER # 47

"**Sincerely**" was sung by The Moonglows. This Louisville group - who were originally called The Crazy Sounds - was renamed by disc jockey Alan Freed. Some of their other hits were: Most of All, See Saw, We Go Together and Please Send Me Someone To Love.

ANSWER # 48

"**Chantilly Lace**" was sung by J. P. "The Big Bopper" Richardson. This disc-jockey/singer from Sabine, Texas named himself after the popular dance craze of the day – the Bop. His second hit was "The Big Bopper's Wedding." He died on Feb. 3rd, 1959 along with Buddy Holly and Richie Valens.

QUESTION # 49

Which group (singer) sang **"At The Hop"**? Was it Bill Haley & The Comets, Danny & The Juniors or The Rascals?

QUESTION # 50

Which group (singer) sang **"Lipstick On Your Collar"**? Was it Leslie Gore, Brenda Lee or Connie Francis?

ANSWER # 49

"**At The Hop**" was sung by Danny & The Juniors. Erroneously, this Philadelphia quartet that was billed as an Italian-American band was led by Danny who was of Irish extraction. Another hit was "Rock and Roll Is Here To Stay." Member, Dave White wrote "You Don't Own Me" (Leslie Gore.)

ANSWER # 50

"**Lipstick On Your Collar**" was sung by Connie Francis (Concetta Rose Maria Franconero). Her unrequited love for singer Bobby Darin resulted from an interfering father and the marriage between Bobby Darin and Sandra Dee. Darin died at age 37 in the recovery room after heart surgery.

QUESTION # 51

Which group (singer) sang **"It's Just A Matter Of Time"**?   Was it Brook Benton, Jerry Butler or Sam Cooke?

QUESTION # 52

Which group (singer) sang **"Teardrops Follow Me"**?   Was it Bobby Darin, Stan Zizka's Del-Satins or Marvin Gaye?

ANSWER # 51

"It's Just A Matter Of Time" was sung by
Brook Benton. Singer/songwriter South
Carolinian Benjamin Franklin Peay co-wrote
this hit and "Endlessly." He also wrote "A
Lover's Question" for Clyde McPhatter.
Other hits included: "A Rainy Night In
Georgia," and "The Boll Weevil Song."

ANSWER # 52

"Teardrops Follow Me" was sung by Stan
Zizka's Del-Satins. When the 2 street corner
groups (the Yorkville Melody & the Jokers)
joined in 1958 and named themselves after
The Dells & The Five Satins, they were led by
Stan Zizka – who later reformed the group
and replaced Johnny Maestro in the Sixties.

QUESTION # 53

Which group (singer) sang **"Stagger Lee"**? Was it Curtis Mayfield, Lloyd Price or Jackie Wilson?

QUESTION # 54

Which group (singer) sang **"Good Timin'"**? Was it Jackie Wilson, Marvin Gaye or Jimmy Jones?

ANSWER # 53

"Stagger Lee" was sung by Lloyd Price. After the Korean War, he returned home to find that he had been replaced on his label by Little Richard. His chauffeur, Larry Williams, was also being recorded. His song was "Short, Fat Fannie." At the end of his career, he managed Southern styled soul foods.

ANSWER # 54

"Good Timin'" was sung by Jimmy Jones. This singer/songwriter African American Alabaman sang in a smooth, yet soulful falsetto. Starting his career as a tap dancer, he joined a doo-wop group known as The Berliners in 1954. His other major hit was "Running Bear."

QUESTION # 55

Which group (singer) sang **"The Stroll"**? Was it The Diamonds, The Dell-Vikings or The Cleftones?

QUESTION # 56

Which group (singer) sang **"The Great Pretender"**? Was it The Temptations, The Platters or The Coasters?

ANSWER # 55

"**The Stroll**" was sung by The Diamonds. When this Canadian group's lead singer, Stan Fisher, was unable to perform one night because of a law exam, their manager, Dave Somerville, replaced him to rave reviews that permanently established the future of the group.

ANSWER # 56

"**The Great Pretender**" was sung by The Platters. Tony Williams and Sonny Turner were the lead singers for this group. Zola Taylor – who was the second of three wives of Frankie Lymon – sang with The Platters from 1954 to 1962 when they had most of their hit singles.

QUESTION # 57

Which group (singer) sang **"Peggy Sue"**?
Was it The Crests, The Byrds or Buddy Holly
& The Crickets?

QUESTION # 58

Which group (singer) sang **"Running Bear"**?
Was it Freddie Cannon, Gene Pitney or
Johnny Preston?

ANSWER # 57

"Peggy Sue" was sung by Buddy Holly & The Crickets. Originally named for Buddy Holly's niece, "Cindy Lou," the song was later changed to its present name because of the temporary breakup of the Cricket's drummer, Jerry Allison, and his girlfriend who eventually became his wife.

ANSWER # 58

"Running Bear" was sung by Johnny Preston. John Preston Courville from Port Arthur, Texas followed this hit with "Cradle of Love." "Running Bear" (1960) was written by J. P. "The Big Bopper" Richardson who had died the year before in 1959 along with Buddy Holly and Richie Valens.

QUESTION # 59

Which group (singer) sang **"Maybellene"**? Was it Johnny Horton, Chuck Berry or Freddie Cannon?

QUESTION # 60

Which group (singer) sang **"Walk, Don't Run"**?   Was it Duane Eddy, Santos & Johnny or The Ventures?

ANSWER # 59

"**Maybellene**" was sung by Chuck Berry. Born to a middle class in St. Louis, Missouri, his first success came after he met Muddy Waters in Chicago and recorded this million-selling hit based on a country song titled "Ida Red." This song reached #1 on Billboard's Rhythm & Blues chart.

ANSWER # 60

"**Walk, Don't Run**" was sung by The Ventures. This instrumental rock band which was formed in 1958 by two masonry workers from Tacoma, Washington, became the best-selling instrumental band of all time. Their influence earned them the moniker "The band that launched a thousand bands."

QUESTION # 61

Which group (singer) sang **"The Green Door"**?   Was it Jim Lowe, Jimmy Clanton or Frankie Avalon?

QUESTION # 62

Which group (singer) sang **"Lonely Boy"**? Was it Jimmy Clanton, Paul Anka or Bobby Helms?

ANSWER # 61

"**The Green Door**" was sung by Jim Lowe. It's lyrics describe a nondescript establishment where the singer is not allowed and where there is a happy crowd who are laughing and smoking. You hear a piano playing in the background. Another song of the era was "Oh Julie" by the Crescendos.

ANSWER # 62

"**Lonely Boy**" was sung by Paul Anka. This Canadian/American singer/songwriter wrote the following: "Diana," "Put Your Head On My Shoulder," and "The Theme From The Tonight Show." He wrote "She's A Lady" (Tom Jones) and "It Doesn't Matter Anymore" (Buddy Holly).

QUESTION # 63

Which group (singer) sang **"Short Shorts"**? Was it The Beach Boys, Jan & Dean or The Royal Teens?

QUESTION # 64

Which group (singer) sang **"Whispering Bells"**? Was it The Dell Vikings, The Students or The Excellents?

ANSWER # 63

"**Short Shorts**" was sung by The Royal Teens. This New Jersey group – originally made up of high school students from Fort Lee High School, All Hallows (Bronx), etc. The title came from cutoff jeans worn by girls during the summer of 1957 whose shortness bordered on being almost illegal.

ANSWER # 64

"**Whispering Bells**" was sung by The Dell Vikings. When the group's manager tried to switch labels because some members of the group were below 21 when they signed a contract, a split occurred that eventually brought about two different groups: the Del-Vikings and the Dell Vikings.

QUESTION # 65

Which group (singer) sang **"Whole Lot Of Shakin' Going On"**?   Was it Chuck Berry, Little Richard or Jerry Lee Lewis?

QUESTION # 66

Which group (singer) sang **"Blue Suede Shoes"**?   Was it Conway Twitty, Roy Orbison or Carl Perkins?

ANSWER # 65

"Whole Lot Of Shakin' Going On" was sung by Jerry Lee Lewis. He was part of the "Million Dollar Quartet" recordings that took place on Tuesday, December 14, 1956 at Sam Phillip's Sun Recording Studio. The other three participants were Elvis Presley, Carl Perkins and Johnny Cash.

ANSWER # 66

"Blue Suede Shoes" was sung by Carl Perkins. This "King of Rockabilly" was one of the "Million Dollar Quartet" at Sam Phillip's Sun Records in Memphis, Tennessee on 12/4/1956. Johnny Cash, Jerry Lee Lewis and Elvis Presley have joined him in the cast of the Broadway play named after them.

QUESTION # 67

Which group (singer) sang **"A White Sports Coat and a Pink Carnation"**?   Was it Marty Robbins, J. P. "The Big Bopper" Richardson or The Four Preps?

QUESTION # 68

Which group (singer) sang **"Don't Let Go"**? Was it Roy Orbinson, Lloyd Price or Roy Hamilton?

ANSWER # 67

"**A White Sports Coat and a Pink Carnation**" was sung by Marty Robbins. This 1957 song (music and lyrics written by him) was inspired by a high school prom attendee he witnessed while driving to a performance. Other #1 recording hits were: "El Paso" and "Big Iron."

ANSWER # 68

"**Don't Let Go**" was sung by Roy Hamilton. This singer from Georgia tried out for the heavyweight Golden Gloves and appeared in a amateur talent show in the Apollo Theater. His most famous hits were: "You Never Walk Alone," "Ebb Tide," "You Can Have Her," and "Unchained Melody."

QUESTION # 69

Which group (singer) sang **"Only The Lonely"**?   Was it Jackie Wilson, Roy Orbinson or Gene Pitney?

QUESTION # 70

Which group (singer) sang **"Kansas City"**? Was it Bobby Helms, Bobby Knox or Wilbert Harrison?

ANSWER # 69

"**Only The Lonely**" was sung by Roy Orbinson. Roy Kelton Orbinson was from Texas. He co-wrote and sang "Blue Bayou." His natural baritone was accompanied by a three or four octave range. He lost his first wife and two sons in separate accidents. In 1988, he died of a heart attack.

ANSWER # 70

"**Kansas City**" was sung by Wilbert Harrison. This North Carolinian singer/pianist/guitarist/harmonica player toured with a band known as the Roamers. Written in 1951, this song is credited with being the first collaboration by the team of Jerry Leiber and Mike Stoller.

QUESTION # 71

Which group (singer) sang **"Goin' Out Of My Head"**?   Was it Frankie Lymon & The Teenagers, Little Anthony & The Imperials or The Dell Vikings?

QUESTION # 72

Which group (singer) sang **"Singing The Blues"**?   Was it Conway Twitty, Guy Mitchell or Roy Orbison?

ANSWER # 71

"Goin' Out Of My Head" was sung by "Little Anthony" & The Imperials. Their list of hits include: "Two Kinds of People," "Shimmy, Shimmy Ko Ko Bop," "Hurt," "Hurt So Bad," "On The Outside (Looking In)," "Take Me Back," and "Out of Sight, Out of Mind."

ANSWER # 72

"Singing The Blues" was sung by Guy Mitchell. Albert George Cernik, who was born of Croatian immigrants in Detroit, Michigan, received his name from Mitch Miller. This song was number one for ten weeks in 1956. It was followed in 1959 by another hit "Heartaches By The Number."

QUESTION # 73

Which group (singer) sang **"Coney Ilsand Baby"**? Was it The Skyliners, The Duprees or the Excellents?

QUESTION # 74

Which group (singer) sang **"Get A Job"**? Was it The Coasters, The Jesters or The Silhouetts?

ANSWER # 73

"Coney Island Baby" was sung by the Excellents. This Bronx sextet formed in 1960 with John Kuse as lead were named the Premiers until renamed the Excellents. Now a quartet, they also recorded: "You Baby You" (Chiffon's hit), "I Hear a Rhapsody," "Helene," and "Sunday Kind of Love."

ANSWER # 74

"Get A Job" was sung by The Silhouetts. The four members from Philadelphia who recorded this song in 1958 took credit for the "sha na na" and "dip dip dip dip" hooks while tenor, Richard Lewis, wrote the lyrics about a nagging mom. Rollie McGill played the saxophone break.

QUESTION # 75

Which group (singer) sang **"Love Is Strange"**?   Was it Duane Eddy, Mickey & Sylvia or The Bell Notes?

QUESTION # 76

Which group (singer) sang **"Diana"**?   Was it Buddy Holly, Tom Jones or Paul Anka?

ANSWER # 75

"**Love Is Strange**" was sung by Mickey & Sylvia. This 1957 song features a sinuous guitar riff and provocative verbal display between Mickey and Sylvia as well as a Latin American beat with a strong melodic hook. The lyrics consist of just eight lines, each of which uses the same basic tune.

ANSWER # 76

"**Diana**" was sung by Paul Anka. This Canadian/American teen idol of the late 1950's co-wrote a few songs with Michael Jackson – "This Is It" and "Love Never Felt So Good". Paul recorded his first single at 14 – it was titled "I Confess." His first hit at 16 was about his babysitter – "Diana."

QUESTION # 77

Which group (singer) sang **"Stay"**?   Was it Maurice Williams & The Zodiacs, The Students or The Excellents?

QUESTION # 78

Which group (singer) sang **"Keep A Knockin'"**?   Was it Chuck Berry, Little Richard or Jackie Wilson?

ANSWER # 77

"**Stay**" was sung by Maurice Williams & The Zodiacs. The Zodiacs began as a gospel group "The Junior Harmonizers," and changed to "The Royal Charms," "The Gladiolas," and finally the "The Exellos." Their "Little Darlin'" rose to #11; the Canadian group, The Diamonds, put it at #2.

ANSWER # 78

"**Keep A Knockin'**" was sung by Little Richard. Richard Wayne Penniman was born in Macon Georgia. This singer/songwriter gospel singer had numerous hits: "Tutti Fruitti," "Long Tall Sally," "Good Golly, Miss Molly," and "Lucille." In 1957, he quit his career to become a born-again Christian.

QUESTION # 79

Which group (singer) sang **"Western Movies"**?   Was it The Coasters, The Jesters or The Olympics?

QUESTION # 80

Which group (singer) sang **"The Happy Organ"**?   Was it Dave "Baby" Cortez, Duane Eddy or The Ventures?

ANSWER # 79

"**Western Movies**" was sung by The Olympics. The Olympics (originally the Challengers) were mostly friends from a Los Angeles high school who recorded this single in 1958. The song reflects the nation's preoccupation with western themed movies and television programs.

ANSWER # 80

"**The Happy Organ**" was sung by Dave "Baby" Cortez. A significant portion of this 1959 instrumental hit bears a strong resemblance to the "Shortening Bread" tune. Unhappy with a recording with lyrics and piano, Cortez brought in an organ which was normally used in the field of jazz.

QUESTION # 81

Which group (singer) sang **"Heartbreak Hotel"**?   Was it Bobby Helms, Elvis Presley or Carl Perkins?

QUESTION # 82

Which group (singer) sang **"Please Let Me Love You"**?   Was it The Jesters, The Paragons, or The Coasters?

ANSWER # 81

"**Heartbreak Hotel**" was sung by Elvis Presley. This best-selling single of 1956 lyrics were based on a newspaper article about the suicide of a lonely man who jumped from a hotel window. Presley recorded at a session that featured his band, The Blue Moon Boys, as well as guitarist, Chet Atkins.

ANSWER # 82

"**Please Let Me Love You**" was sung by The Jesters. As students from Cooper Junior High School in Harlem who sang under a subway el station at 120th Street, they achieved their first success at an Apollo's amateur night. "The Paragons versus The Jesters" album was commercially successful.

QUESTION # 83

Which group (singer) sang **"Lonely Teardrops"**? Was it Jackie Wilson, Marvin Gaye or Lloyd Price?

QUESTION # 84

Which group (singer) sang **"I'm Not Worth It"**? Was it Brenda Lee, Bocky & The Visions or Connie Francis?

ANSWER # 83

"**Lonely Teardrops**" was sung by Jackie Wilson. This song was written by Barry Gordy, Gwendolyn Gordy (Barry's sister) and Roque "Billy" Davis under the pseudonym of Tyran Carlo. Within a year, Barry Gordy was able to found Motown Records from this records success as a number 1 hit.

ANSWER # 84

"**I'm Not Worth It**" was sung by Bocky & The Visions. Bocky was the name used by Robert J. DiPasquale who was the lead singer of this Cleveland vocal group. The group was the opening act for Leslie Gore, The Animals, The Rolling Stones & Dave Clark Five when they appeared in Cleveland.

QUESTION # 85

Which group (singer) sang **"The Battle of New Orleans"**?   Was it Freddie Cannon, or Johnny Horton?

QUESTION # 86

Which group (singer) sang **"Chances Are"**? Was it Johnny Mathis, Pat Boone or Sam Cooke?

ANSWER # 85

"**The Battle of New Orleans**" was sung by Johnny Horton. This Los Angeles-born country music and semi-folk singer started the "saga songs" which became "historical ballads" like "North To Alaska," and "Sink The Bismarck." He had 2 girls with his second wife who was Hank Williams' widow.

ANSWER # 86

"**Chances Are**" was sung by Johnny Mathis. John Royce "Johnny" Mathis was born 4th of 7 children in Gilmer, Texas before his family moved to San Francisco. In high school, he earned four athletic letters and considered entering the Olympics as a high jumper while attending college as an English major.

QUESTION # 87

Which group (singer) sang **"The Three Bells"**? Was it The Fleetwoods, The Browns or The Kalin Twins?

QUESTION # 88

Which group (singer) sang **"Sleep Walk"**? Was it Mickey & Sylvia, Duane Eddy or Santo & Johnny?

ANSWER # 87

"**The Three Bells**" was sung by The Browns. This 1959 hit based on a 1945 French language song had numerous recorded versions. In 1959, it was #1 on the country and pop song chart, while reaching number 10 on the Hot R&B Sides chart. It is referred to as "Little Jimmy Brown" at times.

ANSWER # 88

"**Sleep Walk**" was sung by Santo & Johnny. The Farina brothers from Brooklyn, NY comprise this duo. Santo played on a steel guitar while Johnny played an acoustic guitar. Today, Santo is semi-retired while Johnny tours, records new material (his own band) and runs an international record company.

QUESTION # 89

Which group (singer) sang **"In The Still Of The Night"**?   Was it The Capris, The Five Satins or The Platters?

QUESTION # 90

Which group (singer) sang **"So Fine"**?   Was it The Turbans, The Fiestas or The Chiffons?

ANSWER # 89

"**In The Still Of The Night**" was sung by The Five Satins. This New Haven, Connecticut group formed in 1954 with Fred Parris as lead singer. When he entered the Army, Bill Baker took his place and "To The Aisle" became a hit. In the early seventies, the group reverted to Fred Parris as lead.

ANSWER # 90

"**So Fine**" was sung by The Fiestas. This Newark, NJ group was discovered singing in a bathroom adjacent to the Harlem office of a record producer. A series of soul singles followed this debut song – only "Broken Heart" managed to reach the charts by scoring #18 on the Black Singles chart..

QUESTION # 91

Which group (singer) sang **"16 candles"**? Was it The Skyliners, Neil Sedaka or The Crests?

QUESTION # 92

Which group (singer) sang **"When You Dance"**?   Was it The Turbans, The Coasters or The Jesters?

ANSWER # 91

"**16 Candles**" was sung by The Crests. This interracial group had three African Americans (one female), one Puerto Rican, and one Italian American member(s). Johnny Mastrangelo (Johnny Maestro) was chosen as lead vocalist. Later, he would solo and also lead a group known as The Brooklyn Bridge.

ANSWER # 92

"**When You Dance**" was sung by The Turbans. In 1955, this African American downtown Philadelphia doo-wop group recorded the song "Let Me Show You (Around My Heart)" as the A-Side with this song on the flip side. Eventually, it hit #3 on the R&B chart and stayed for two months.

QUESTION # 93

Which group (singer) sang **"Rebel Rouser"**? Was it The Ventures, Duane Eddy & The Rebels or The Champs?

QUESTION # 94

Which group (singer) sang **"A Thousand Stars"**? Was it Brenda Lee, Leslie Gore or Kathy Young & The Innocents?

ANSWER # 93

"**Rebel Rouser**" was sung by Duane Eddy & The Rebels. Corning, New York born Duane Eddy began playing the guitar at the age of five. Eventually, his family relocated to Arizona where he formed his own group, The Rebels. Using the bass on his guitar, he was able to create his low "twangy" sound.

ANSWER # 94

"**A Thousand Stars**" was sung by Kathy Young & The Innocents. In 1960, a record producer named Jim Lee paired up Kathy Young with The Innocents to do this song which had been performed earlier in 1954 by a group called The Rivileers. She was only 15. She later married and lives in London.

QUESTION # 95

Which group (singer) sang **"Raunchy"**? Was it The Ventures, Duane Eddy & The Rebels or The Champs?

QUESTION # 96

Which group (singer) sang **"Heartaches By The Number"**?   Was it Conway Twitty, Guy Mitchell or Roy Orbison?

ANSWER # 95

"**Raunchy**" was sung by Duane Eddy & The Rebels. Working with DJ/Record Producer Lee Hazelwood, Duane Eddy performed inside an empty 2000 gallon water storage tank in the recording studio in order to create the low, reverberating "twangy" sound that also made him famous on "Peter Gunn."

ANSWER # 96

"**Heartaches By The Number**" was sung by Guy Mitchell. Albert George Cernik, who was born of Croatian immigrants in Detroit, Michigan, received his name from Mitch Miller. George Jones did his version on his 1961 album. This 1959 hit was preceded by his 1956 hit, "Singing The Blues."

QUESTION # 97

Which group (singer) sang **"A Teenager In Love"**?   Was it Frankie Lymon & The Teenagers, Little Anthony & The Imperials or Dion & The Belmonts?

QUESTION # 98

Which group (singer) sang **"Venus"**?   Was it Frankie Avalon, Fabian or Ricky Nelson?

ANSWER # 97

"**A Teenager In Love**" was sung by Dion &
The Belmonts. In March 1959, it was
released and reached #5 on the Billboard pop
charts. In 1970, it was sung by Simon &
Garfunkel in their last show which was held
at Forest Hills Tennis Stadium in Queens,
New York.

ANSWER # 98

"**Venus**" was sung by Frankie Avalon. This
actor/singer was the most successful teen
idol from Philadelphia. Married in 1963, he is
the father of eight children and ten
grandchildren. Along with the hit, 'Why," in
1959, he has acted in a number of "beach"
comedy movies with Annette Funicello

QUESTION # 99

Which group (singer) sang **"Wake Up Little Susie"**?   Was it The Kalin Twins, The Everly Brothers or Chuck Berry?

QUESTION # 100

Which group (singer) sang **" I'm Not A Juvenile Delinquent "**?   Was it Little Anthony & The Imperials, Frankie Lymon & The Teenagers or The Students?

ANSWER # 99

"**Wake Up Little Susie**" was sung by The Everly Brothers. Issac Donald Everly was born in Kentucky while the younger Phillip was born two years later in Chicago, IL. Don sang the lower harmony while Phil sang the higher. Don almost always sang any solo lines. They played steel-string guitars.

ANSWER # 100

"**I'm Not A Juvenile Delinquent**" was sung by Frankie Lymon & The Teenagers. After Diana Ross returned "Why Do Fools Fall In Love" back to the Top Ten in 1981, a probate challenge occurred between three women: Zola Taylor (singer with the Platters), Elizabeth Waters and Emira Eagle.

QUESTION # 101

Which group (singer) sang **"Hushabye"**? Was it The Mystics, The Capris or The Monotones?

QUESTION # 102

Which group (singer) sang **"Mr. Blue"**? Was it The Browns, The Fleetwoods or The Kalin Twins?

ANSWER # 101

"Hushabye" was sung by The Mystics. This Brooklyn quintet known as the Overons chose their new name by picking names out of a hat. With a number of lead singer changes, Paul Simon (aka Jerry Landis) was one.

ANSWER # 102

"Mr. Blue" was sung by The Fleetwoods. This Olympia, WA trio (originally called Two Girls and a Guy) changed the name of their group and the name of their first song, "Come Softly," on the way to becoming a chart topper. "Come Softly To Me" was the first of eleven hits.

QUESTION # 103

Which group (singer) sang **"Young Love"**?
Was it Pat Boone, Fabian or Sonny James?

QUESTION # 104

Which group (singer) sang **"Tequila"**?   Was
it The Champs, The Ventures or The Bell
Notes?

ANSWER # 103

"**Young Love**" was sung by Sonny James.
This song was released in 1957 and was also
recorded by Tab Hunter and The Crew-Cuts.
On the Disc Jockey chart, it peaked at #1; on
the Best Seller chart, it was #2; on the Juke
Box chart, it was #4; and on the composite
chart of the top 100 songs, it reached #2.

ANSWER # 104

"**Tequila**" was sung by The Champs. As the
flip side of a single in 1958, this song went to
#1 in just 3 weeks and the band became the
first group to go to the top with an
instrumental as their 1st release. The Champs
also had instrumental hits with such singles as
"Limbo Rock" and "La Cucharacha."

Which group (singer) sang **"Long Tall Sally"**?   Was it Jackie Wilson,, Little Richard or Jimmy Jones?

QUESTION # 106

Which group (singer) sang **"Rock And Roll Is Here To Stay"**?   Was it The Rascals, The Olympics or Danny & The Juniors?

ANSWER # 105

"**Long Tall Sally**" was sung by Little Richard. Richard Wayne Penniman was born in Macon Georgia. This singer/songwriter gospel singer had numerous hits: "Tutti Fruitti," "Long Tall Sally," "Good Golly, Miss Molly," and "Lucille." He was born the third of twelve siblings.

ANSWER # 106

"**Rock And Roll Is Here To Stay**" was sung by Danny & The Juniors. This Philadelphia quartet which formed in 1955 also recorded "Twistin' USA" which charted in the Top 40. Member Dave White wrote "1-2-3" and "Like A Baby" for Len Barry and "You Don't Own Me" for Leslie Gore.

QUESTION # 107

Which group (singer) sang **"Tonight's The Night"**?   Was it The Chiffons, The Velvets or Leslie Gore?

QUESTION # 108

Which group (singer) sang **"You're So Fine"**?   Was it The Shirelles, The Falcons or Martha & The Vandellas?

ANSWER # 107

"**Tonight's The Night**" was sung by The Chiffons. This female vocal group formed in 1960 at James Monroe High School with 14 year old Judy Craig as lead singer.
Subsequent hits were: "One Fine Day," "I Have A Boyfriend," "Sailor Boy," and "Sweet Talkin' Guy."

ANSWER # 108

"**You're So Fine**" was sung by The Falcons. This American rhythm and blues vocal group was formed in 1955 in Detroit, Michigan. They recorded this million selling single in 1959. One of their claims to fame was that during all the turnovers they had with members, Wilson Pickett sung with them.

QUESTION # 109

Which group (singer) sang **"Ain't That A Shame"**?   Was it Lloyd Price, Jackie Wilson or Fats Domino?

QUESTION # 110

Which group (singer) sang **"C'Mon Everybody"**?   Was it Eddie Cochran, Conway Twitty or Carl Perkins?

ANSWER # 109

"**Ain't That A Shame**" was sung by Fats Domino. This Louisianan, singer/songwriter pianist Antoine Dominique "Fats" Domino crossed over into the pop mainstream with this single in 1955. "Fats" Domino eventually had 37 Top 40 singles after this single was released.

ANSWER # 110

"**C'Mon Everybody**" was sung by Eddie Cochran. This American rockabilly artist was killed in 1960 at the age of 21 while on a British tour. His other notable hits were "Summertime Blues," and "Somethin' Else." During his lifetime, he experimented with multitracking and overdubbing on his songs.

QUESTION # 111

Which group (singer) sang **"Eddie My Love"**?   Was it The Shirelles, The Chordettes or The Chiffons?

QUESTION # 112

Which group (singer) sang **"Turn Me Loose"**?   Was it Frankie Avalon, Bobby Darin or Fabian?

ANSWER # 111

"**Eddie My Love**" was sung by The Chordettes. This song was also recorded by The Teen Queens. The Chordettes were a female quartet that usually sang a cappella. Besides "Eddie My Love," their version of "Lollipop," made #2 in 1958 and became their most successful hit.

ANSWER # 112

"**Turn Me Loose**" was sung by Fabian. Fabiano Anthony Forte was a South Philadelphia, PA teen idol with eleven songs that reached the Billboard Hot 100 listing. Some of his hits were: "I'm A Man," "Hound Dog Man," and his biggest hit "Tiger" which was number three in the U.S.

QUESTION # 113

Which group (singer) sang **"Little Bitty Pretty One"**?   Was it Little Richard, Jerry Lee Lewis or Thurston Harris?

QUESTION # 114

Which group (singer) sang **"Be-Bop-A-Lula"**?   Was it Freddie Cannon, Little Richard or Gene Vincent & His Blue Caps?

ANSWER # 113

"Little Bitty Pretty One" was sung by Thurston Harris. This singer first appeared on a record as the featured vocalist for the Lamplighters in 1953 during the early R&B scene in South Central Los Angeles. His one-hit wonder that he recorded in 1957 with The Sharps and reached #6 on the charts.

ANSWER # 114

"**Be-Bop-A-Lula**" was sung by Gene Vincent & His Blue Caps. Blue Caps were enlisted sailors at that time – now they are referred to as White Hats. After his leg injury (motorcycle accident), he left the service. "Lotta Lovin'" (1957) was before his movie The Girl Can't Help It – Jayne Mansfield.

QUESTION # 115

Which group (singer) sang **"Ten Commandments of Love"**?   Was it The Moonglows, The Monotones or The Coasters?

QUESTION # 116

Which group (singer) sang **"Blueberry Hill"**? Was it The Everly Brothers, Fats Domino or Freddie Cannon?

ANSWER # 115

"**Ten Commandments of Love**" was sung by The Moonglows. Formed in Kentucky, this group moved to Cleveland where they were given their name by DJ Alan Freed after his nickname "Moondog." This song was the group's number two single's hit after their number one hit "Sincerely."

ANSWER # 116

"**Blueberry Hill**" was sung by Fats Domino. This 1956 hit was followed by such hits as: "When My Dreamboat Comes Home," "I'm Walkin," "Valley Of Tears," "It's You I Love," "Whole Lotta Loving," "I Want To Walk You Home," "Be My Guest," and "Walkin To New Orleans."

QUESTION # 117

Which group (singer) sang **"Moovin' n' Groovin'"**?   Was it Johnny Horton, The Ventures or Duane Eddy & The Rebels?

QUESTION # 118

Which group (singer) sang **"Johnny B. Goode"**?   Was it Little Richard, Chuck Berry or Jerry Lee Lewis?

ANSWER # 117

"**Moovin' n' Groovin'**" was sung by Duane
Eddy. This 1957 recording was the first by
Duane Eddy and his band. Other singles that
followed this instrumental co-written with
Lee Hazelwood were as follows: "Peter
Gunn", "Cannonball", "Shazam" and "Forty
Miles Of Bad Road."

ANSWER # 118

"**Johnny B. Goode**" was sung by Chuck
Berry. Before his 1st hit, "Maybellene," he
spent time in prison and worked as a family
man in the automotive industry. After
achieving success, he owned a nightclub
called Berry's Club Bandstand and spent time
in prison under the Mann Act.

QUESTION # 119

Which group (singer) sang **"Poor Little Fool"**?   Was it Frankie Avalon, Ricky Nelson or Fabian?

QUESTION # 120

Which group (singer) sang **"Come Softly To Me"**?   Was it Dion, Gene Pitney or The Fleetwoods?

ANSWER # 119

"**Poor Little Fool**" was sung by Ricky Nelson. Teen idol Eric Hilliard Nelson recorded this hit in 1958 and sang it on his family TV program. Married in 1963, Nelson had four children before divorcing in 1982. While engaged to another woman, he died in an tragic airplane crash in 1985.

ANSWER # 120

"**Come Softly To Me**" was sung by The Fleetwoods. One of two Olympic High School students humming a jazz trumpet riff reminded a girl of a chord progression she was working on for a song she was writing. Joined by another girl, they put together this song while shaking car keys for rhythm.

QUESTION # 121

Which group (singer) sang **"Gone"**?   Was it Ferlin Husky, Johnny Cash or Tennessee Ernie Ford?

QUESTION # 122

Which group (singer) sang **"Teen Beat"**? Was it Duane Eddy, Sandy Nelson or The Champs?

ANSWER # 121

"**Gone**" was sung by Ferlin Husky. This song and "Wings of a Dove" both reached #1 on the country charts. In 1957, "Gone" was a crossover hit on the pop music chart at #4. This Missourian singer had served aboard merchant marine ships – even one that participated in the D-Day invasion.

ANSWER # 122

"**Teen Beat**" was sung by Sandy Nelson. This Californian drummer went to high school with Jan and Dean. He played drums for Phil Spector's Teddy Bears on "To Know Him Is To Love Him," The Hollywood Argyles' "Alley-Oop," and Kathy Young and The Innocents' "A Thousand Stars."

QUESTION # 123

Which group (singer) sang **"Willie And The Hand Jive"**?   Was it Johnny Otis, Johnny & The Hurricanes or Johnny Horton?

QUESTION # 124

Which group (singer) sang **"Mule Skinner Blues"**?   Was it The Fendermen, Duane Eddy or The Ventures?

ANSWER #123

"**Willie And The Hand Jive**" was sung by Johnny Otis. John Alexander Veliotis is a rhythm and blues, pianist, composer, drummer, singer, band leader and impresario who was born of Greek immigrants. His older brother was US Ambassador to Jordan and Egypt during the 1970's and 1980's.

ANSWER # 124

"**Mule Skinner Blues**" was sung by The Fendermen. This group was primarily formed by two students attending the University of Wisconsin-Madison. One was from Michigan and the other was from Wisconsin. They named the group after the Fender guitars they plugged into one amp.

QUESTION # 125

Which group (singer) sang **"The Book of Love"**? Was it The Marcels, The Moonglows or The Monotones?

QUESTION # 126

Which group (singer) sang **"Gloria"**? Was it The Cadillacs, Vito and the Salutations or The Passions?

ANSWER # 125

"**The Book of Love**" was sung by The Monotones. This six member Newark vocal group began singing with the New Hope Baptist choir. When they recorded this one-hit wonder in 1958, it was a sextet. All of the members were residents of the Baxter Terrace housing project in Newark.

ANSWER # 126

"**Gloria**" was sung by all three of these groups plus about 47 other groups. While The Cadillacs were the most popular group in terms of sales, there were other good versions by The Five Thrills and The Chariots.

QUESTION # 127

Which group (singer) sang **"Why Do Fools Fall In Love"**? Was it Smoky Robinson & The Miracles, Frankie Lymon & The Teenagers or Little Anthony & The Imperials?

QUESTION # 128

Which group (singer) sang **"Since I Met You Baby"**? Was it Lenny Welch, The Skyliners or Ivory Joe Hunter?

ANSWER # 127

"**Why Do Fools Fall In Love**" was sung by Frankie Lymon & The Teenagers. This New York City interracial quintet of early to mid-teens was comprised of three African American members and two Puerto Rican members. Frankie Lymon died of a heroin overdose at the age of 25.

ANSWER # 128

"**Since I Met You Baby**" was sung by Ivory Joe Hunter. Christened Ivory Joe, this Texan singer/songwriter/pianist was billed as The Baron of the Boogie and The Happiest Man Alive. After recording this song in 1956, he visited Memphis, Tennessee where he spent a day at Graceland singing with Elvis Presley.

QUESTION # 129

Which group (singer) sang **"Jim Dandy"**? Was it Jackie Wilson, Lloyd Price or LaVern Baker?

QUESTION # 130

Which group (singer) sang **"Maybe"**? Was it The "Original" Chantels, The Shirelles or Martha & The Vandellas?

ANSWER # 129

"**Jim Dandy**" was sung by LaVern Baker.
Early in her career in her native Chicago, she
was billed in clubs as Little Miss
Sharecropper. After her 1956 hit, "Tweedlee
Dee," she had this hit. It was followed by
"Jim Dandy Got Married," and "I Waited
Too Long" (written by Neil Sedaka).

ANSWER # 130

"**Maybe**" was sung by The "Original"
Chantels. They were the second African
American girl group to have nationwide
success. The group was formed at St.
Anthony of Padua School in the Bronx, NY.
In time, the lead singer, Arlene Smith, was
replaced by Annette Smith (no relation).

QUESTION # 131

Which group (singer) sang **"Put Your Head On My Shoulder"**? Was it Paul Anka, Pat Boone or Frankie Avalon?

QUESTION # 132

Which group (singer) sang **"Splish Splash"**? Was it The Coasters, Bobby Darin or The Big Bopper?

ANSWER # 131

"**Put Your Head On My Shoulder**" was
sung by Paul Anka. This Canadian born
singer/songwriter wrote the following:
"Diana," "Put Your Head On My Shoulder,"
and "The Theme From The Tonight Show."
He wrote "She's A Lady" (Tom Jones) and
"It Doesn't Matter Anymore" (Buddy Holly).

ANSWER # 132

"**Splish Splash**" was sung by Bobby Darin.
Walden Robert Perciville Cassotto was born
into a poor working class family of Italian
descent. Always hampered by fragile health,
he became a goodwill ambassador to The
American Heart Society. He anticipated a
short life and actually died at 37 years of age.

QUESTION # 133

Which group (singer) sang **"Great Balls of Fire"**? Was it Little Richard, Jerry Lee Lewis or Chuck Berry?

QUESTION # 134

Which group (singer) sang **"Charlie Brown"**? Was it The Jesters, The Paragons or The Coasters?

ANSWER # 133

"**Great Balls of Fire**" was sung by Jerry Lee Lewis. Jerry Lee was born into a poor family in Louisiana where he played piano at a young age with his two cousins, Jimmy Swaggart and Mickey Gilley – both of whom were to become famous in their own right. He went to Memphis, TN in 1956.

ANSWER # 134

"**Charlie Brown**" was sung by The Coasters. The Coasters were formed as a Los Angeles rhythm and blues group named The Robins. Their association with the songwriting and producing team of Leiber and Stroller in Los Angeles led to their move to New York in 1955 as a doo-wop group.

QUESTION # 135

Which group (singer) sang **"Tossin' & Turnin'"**?   Was it Bobby Knox, Bobby Lewis or Bobby Darin?

QUESTION # 136

Which group (singer) sang **"Let's Start Over Again"**?   Was it Frankie Lymon & the Teenagers, The Cleftones or The Paragons?

ANSWER # 135

"**Tossin' & Turnin'**" was sung by Bobby Lewis. Born in Indiana, this African American rock and roll and R&B singer learned to play the piano by age 6. Adopted at age 12, he moved to a home in Detroit, Michigan. After this song reached #1, he only had one other hit – "One Track Mind."

ANSWER # 136

"**Let's Start Over Again**" was sung by The Paragons. This Brooklyn vocal group was formed in 1955. Their first hit was labeled "Florence/Hey Little School Girl" and it hit the charts in 1957. Two further hits were "Two Hearts Are Better Than One" and "Twilight."

QUESTION # 137

Which group (singer) sang **"Searchin'"**? Was it The Jesters, The Coasters or The Paragons?

QUESTION # 138

Which group (singer) sang **"Just a Dream"**? Was it Jimmy Clanton, Conway Twitty or Gene Pitney?

ANSWER # 137

"**Searchin'**" was sung by The Coasters. Other best selling hits by this group include: "Young Blood," "Yakety Yak," "Along Came Jones," "Charlie Brown," "Poison Ivy," and "Love Potion #9." Members were constantly coming and going. One member was Earl "Speedo" Carroll from The Cadillacs.

ANSWER # 138

"**Just a Dream**" was sung by Jimmy Clanton. This song was written by this Louisianan was known as the 'swamp pop R&B teenage idol." He formed his first band called The Rockets in 1956. After being drafted, his success continued with such hits as: "Because I Do," and "Venus in Blue Jeans."

QUESTION # 139

Which group (singer) sang **"Since I Don't Have You"**? Was it The Skyliners, Lenny Welch or Ivory Joe Hunter?

QUESTION # 140

Which group (singer) sang **"Goody Goody"**? Was it "Little" Anthony & The Imperials, Frankie Lymon & The Teenagers or The Students?

ANSWER # 139

"**Since I Don't Have You**" was sung by The Skyliners. This Pittsburg quintet featured Jimmy Beaumont as lead along with three males and Janet Vogel. Other Top 40 hits by the Skyliners were "This I Swear," "Pennies from Heaven," "Close Your Eyes" and "It Happened Today."

ANSWER # 140

"**Goody Goody**" was sung by Frankie Lymon & The Teenagers. Their hits include: "I Want You To Be My Girl," "I Promise To Remember," "Who Can Explain," "Out In The Cold Again," "The ABC's Of Love," "I'm Not A Juvenile Delinquent," "Baby Baby," and "I Want You To Be My Girl."

QUESTION # 141

Which group (singer) sang **"For Your Precious Love"**? Was it Tommy Edwards, Sam Cooke or Jerry Butler & The Impressions?

QUESTION # 142

Which group (singer) sang **"Mr. Lee"**? Was it The Bobbettes, The Shirelles or Marta and the Vandellas?

ANSWER # 141

"**For Your Precious Love**" was sung by Jerry Butler & The Impressions. Aside from being the original lead singer for the Impressions, this Mississippi-born singer/songwriter sang in a church choir with Curtis Mayfield. Later in life, he was elected as Commissioner of Cook County, IL and other chairmanships.

ANSWER # 142

"**Mr. Lee**" was sung by The Bobbettes. This group formed in Harlem in 1955 when they met at P.S. 109's Glee Club. Originally, they were called The Harlem Queens. Their discovery was at an Apollo Theater amateur night. They were the first girl group to release a #1 R&B that made pop Top Ten.

QUESTION # 143

Which group (singer) sang **"Bye Bye Love"**? Was it The Kalin Twins, The Everly Brothers or Chuck Berry?

QUESTION # 144

Which group (singer) sang **"La Bamba"**? Was it The Champs, Richie Valens or Buddy Holly?

ANSWER # 143

"**Bye Bye Love**" was sung by The Everly Brothers. The brothers sang simple vocal harmony based on parallel thirds. While each of their melody lines would stand on its own, classic harmony working alongside melody do not. Touring extensively with Buddy Holly in 1957-58, Phil was pallbearer at his funeral.

ANSWER # 144

"**La Bamba**" was sung by Richie Valens (born Ricardo Esteban Valenzuela Reyes). Leading the Chicano rock movement, his hit song "La Bamba" is a Mexican folk song with a rock rhythm. His career ended on Feb. 3rd, 1959 along with Buddy Holly and J. P. "The Big Bopper" Richardson in a plane crash.

QUESTION # 145

Which group (singer) sang **"Dream Lover"**?
Was it Sam Cooke, Bobby Darin or the
Everly Brothers?

QUESTION # 146

Which group (singer) sang **"I Only Have
Eyes For You"**?   Was it The Turbans, The
Crests or The Flamingos?

ANSWER # 145

"**Dream Lover**" was sung by Bobby Darin. This singer/actor/accomplished musician attended the prestigious Bronx High School of Science and Hunter College on a scholarship. He left Hunter College to play small nightclubs in the city. He was married to actress Sandra Dee and they had a son.

ANSWER # 146

"**I Only Have Eyes For You**" was sung by The Flamingos. This Chicagoan sextet had numerous names prior to this one: The Swallows, El Flamingos and The Five Flamingos. An original member has spent the last 50 years with The Dells after his discharge from the armed services.

QUESTION # 147

Which group (singer) sang **"Do You Wanna Dance?"**? Was it Bobby Helms, Bobby Knox or Bobby Freeman?

QUESTION # 148

Which group (singer) sang **"Save the Last Dance For Me"**? Was it The Drifters, The Elegants or The Five Satins?

ANSWER # 147

"**Do You Wanna Dance?**" was sung by Bobby Freeman. This African American singer/songwriter/record producer sang this hit in 1958 at age 17. His 1964 Top Ten hit "C'mon And Swim" was written by 20 year old Slyvester Stewart later known as Sly Stone. The follow-up was "S-W-I-M."

ANSWER # 148

"**Save the Last Dance For Me**" was sung by The Drifters. Besides splinter groups, there have been 60 vocalists in the Treadwell Drifter group between 1953 and 1963. The two most notable lead singers for the Drifters have been Clyde McPhatter (from Bill Ward & The Dominoes) and Ben E. King.

QUESTION # 149

Which group (singer) sang **"Blue Moon**"? Was it The Marcels, Mitch Ryder and the Detroit Wheels or Duane Eddy?

QUESTION # 150

Which group (singer) sang **"A Lover's Question"**? Was it Jackie Wilson, Clyde McPhatter or Tommy Edwards?

ANSWER # 149

"**Blue Moon**" was sung by The Marcels. This Pittsburgh group was named after Fred Johnson's haircut – the marcel. The Marcels also had another Top Ten single called "Heartaches."

ANSWER # 150

"**A Lover's Question**" was sung by Clyde McPhatter. Viewed as a key figure in the shaping of doo-wop and R&B, this North Carolinian founder of The Drifters also wrote one of their first hits, "Lucille." He was replaced on The Dominoes by lead singer, Jackie Wilson. He died at the early age of 39.

Made in the USA
Charleston, SC
19 May 2011